The Healthy

medic food for life

Easy **15 minute recipe book** to help
you live well every day with low calorie
meals in 15 minutes or less

Meals in
15
minutes

THE HEALTHY MEDIC FOOD FOR LIFE
EASY 15 MINUTE RECIPE BOOK TO HELP YOU LIVE WELL
EVERY DAY WITH LOW-CALORIE MEALS IN 15 MINUTES OR LESS

ISBN: 978-1-913005-23-8

• •

DISCLAIMER

CONTENTS

DINNER

CONVERSION CHART

OTHER TITLES

INTRODUCTION

If you are time-poor but want to eat healthy, delicious, nutritious meals every day…. you can, and all in 15 minutes or less!

In our fast paced way of life, healthy, balanced and nutritious meals are often the first thing to be compromised. "I haven't got time to cook", "I'll eat on the go" or "I'll skip lunch and eat later" are just some of the excuses we all use throughout our hectic lives resulting in poor diet choices, sluggishness and weight gain.

If you are following a diet, meal choices can become even more difficult and the added pressure of finding time to prepare food can cause you to fall at the first hurdle.

Here's the good news. If you are time-poor but want to eat healthy, delicious and nutritious meals every day… you can, and all in 15 minutes or less! The Healthy Medic Food For Life Recipe Book brings 70 breakfast, lunch and dinner recipes to the table in 15 minutes or less and all below 300, 400 or 500 calories each.

Each recipe serves two and is big on flavour and nutrition – no compromises.

If you think you haven't got time to cook…think again. You could be eating delicious, skinny, fat burning meals every day in just 15 minutes.

THE SECRET TO 15 MINUTE MEALS

Preparing and cooking meals in 15 minutes or less requires a little help from modern convenience stores in the shape of some carefully selected pre-prepared products. Slashing prep times is how you can make 15 minutes meals in a flash.

By altering your shopping habits a little, your fridge and store cupboard can be regularly stocked with super-fast pre-prepared ingredients that make meals simple – less time, less fuss, less washing up! We're not talking highly processed fast food but instead, freshly prepared ingredients that will save you the time chopping, washing, peeling, grating and all the other laborious tasks that add minutes to your kitchen prep.

To follow is a list of some of the most common pre-prepared smart buys used in our recipes that will slash time off your cooking. This is not however a comprehensive shopping list, so check which recipes you plan to follow and shop accordingly.

- Jar of sliced prepared ginger
- Jar of crushed prepared garlic
- Jar crushed chilli flakes
- Bags pre sliced/chopped onions
- Bags pre sliced/chopped red onions
- Bags prepared carrot batons
- Bags washed, sliced mushrooms
- Bags washed rocket, spinach and mixed salad leaves
- Bags prepared shredded kale & spring greens
- Packets trimmed asparagus tips
- Packets trimmed green beans

- Packets shelled fresh peas
- Pre-grated low fat cheddar cheese
- Pre-grated Parmesan cheese
- Packets straight-to-wok noodles
- Packets ready-to-go microwaveable rice
- Bottle of lime juice
- Bottle of lemon juice
- Jar sundried tomatoes in oil
- Cubed pancetta
- Curry powder
- Pre-cooked chicken breasts

Remember that pre-prepared just means someone has already done some of the work for you. The ingredients we suggest are still nutritious, fresh and full of flavour – no compromises on taste or goodness. Adding these items may add a few extra pennies to your weekly shopping budget but the time you will save in the kitchen will be worth it. Plus you will eating great-tasting, healthy, calorie counted meals every day…in just 15 minutes.

You could of course prepare many of these ingredients yourself when you have more time and have them ready in the fridge to use when preparing your 15 minute meals.

LOW CALORIE RECIPES

The recipes in this book are all low calorie dishes for two, which will make it easier for you to monitor your overall daily calorie intake as well as those you are cooking for. The recommended daily calories are approximately 2000 for women and 2500 for men.

Broadly speaking, by consuming the recommended levels of calories each day you should maintain your current weight. Reducing the number of calories (a calorie deficit) will result in losing weight. This happens because the body begins to use fat stores for energy to make up the reduction in calories, which in turn results in weight loss. We have already counted the calories for each dish making it easy for you to fit this into your daily eating plan whether you want to lose weight, maintain your current figure or are just looking for some great-tasting, comforting, winter warming recipes.

I'M ALREADY ON A DIET. CAN I USE THESE RECIPES?

Yes of course. All the recipes can be great accompaniments to many of the popular calorie-counting diets. We all know that sometimes dieting can result in hunger pangs, cravings and boredom from eating the same old foods day in and day out. The Healthy Medic Food For Life meals provide filling recipes which should satisfy you for hours afterwards.

I AM ONLY COOKING FOR ONE. WILL THIS BOOK WORK FOR ME?

Yes. We would recommend following the method for two servings then dividing and storing the rest for you to use another day. You will find one or two recipes in this book which are single servings.

PREPARATION & COOKING TIMES

All the recipes should take no longer than 15 minutes to prepare and cook. This is based on making full use of our suggestions for some pre-prepared ingredients. If you prefer to prepare your ingredients from scratch then obviously allow longer prep time.

All meat should be trimmed of visible fat and the skin removed.

All the recipes in this book are a guide only. You may need to alter quantities and cooking times to suit your own appliances.

NUTRITION

All of the recipes in this collection are balanced low calorie meals which should keep you feeling full. It is important to balance your food between proteins, good carbs, dairy, fruit and vegetables.

Protein. Keeps you feeling full and is also essential for building body tissue. Good protein sources come from meat, fish and eggs.

Carbohydrates. Not all carbs are good and generally they are high in calories, which makes them difficult to include in a calorie limiting diet. However carbs are a good source of energy for your body as they are converted more easily into glucose (sugar) providing energy. Try to eat 'good carbs' which are high in fibre and nutrients e.g. whole fruits and veg, nuts, seeds, whole grain cereals, beans and legumes.

Good Fats. A small amount of fat is an essential part of a healthy, balanced diet. Fat is a source of essential fatty acids such as omega-3 – "essential" because the body can't make them itself. Fat helps the body absorb vitamins A, D and E. Good fats can be found in olive oil, rapeseed oil, avocados, almond nuts and oily fish such as sardines, salmon and tuna.

Dairy. Dairy products provide you with vitamins and minerals. Cheeses can be very high in calories but other products such as low fat Greek yoghurt, crème fraiche and skimmed milk are all good.

Fruit & Vegetables. Eat your five a day. There is never a better time to fill your 5 a day quota. Not only are fruit and veg very healthy, they also fill up your plate and are ideal snacks when you are feeling hungry.

PORTION SIZES

The size of the portion that you put on your plate will significantly affect your weight loss efforts. Filling your plate with over-sized portions will obviously increase your calorie intake and hamper your dieting efforts.

It's important with all meals that you use a correct sized portion, which generally is the size of your clenched fist. This applies to any side dishes of vegetables and carbs too.

The portion sizes in our 15 minute meal recipes are the correct size for the average adult but remember that each recipe serves two so don't be tempted to over-fill your plate if you are cooking just for one!

MEASUREMENTS

All recipes are for two servings but can easily be increased if you are cooking for more people. As with portion sizes, stick with the recommended measurements of ingredients. Altering these will affect your calorie intake and therefore your ultimate weight loss.

WEIIGHT LOSS TIPS

If you are following a diet or generally keeping an eye on your calorie intake, here are some tips that will help you manage the way you eat.

In today's fast moving society many of use have adopted an unhealthy habit of eating. We eat as quickly as possibly without properly giving our bodies the chance to digest and feel full. Not only is this bad for your digestive system, but our bodies begin to relate food to just fuel instead of actually enjoying what we are eating.

Some simple tips for eating which may help you on your fasting days:

·   Eat. Take it slow. There is no rush.
·   Chew. It sounds obvious but you should properly chew your food and swallow only when it's broken down and you have enjoyed what you have tasted.
·   Wait. Before reaching for second helpings wait 5-10 minutes and let your body tell you whether you are still hungry. More often than not, the answer will be no and you will be satisfied with the meal you have had. A glass of water before each meal will help you with any cravings for more.
·   Avoid alcohol when you can. Alcohol is packed with calories and will counter affect any calorific reduction you are practising with your daily meals.
·   Drink plenty of water throughout the day. It's good for you, has zero calories, and will fill you up and help stop you feeling hungry.
·   Drink a glass of water before and also with your meal. Again this will help you feel fuller.
·   When you are eating each meal, put your fork down between bites – it will make you eat more slowly and you'll feel fuller on less food.

- Brush your teeth immediately after your meal to discourage yourself from eating more.
- If unwanted food cravings do strike, acknowledge them, then distract yourself. Go out for a walk, phone a friend, play with the kids, or paint your nails.
- Whenever hunger hits, try waiting 15 minutes and ride out the cravings. You'll find they pass and you can move on with your day.
- Remember - feeling a bit hungry is not a bad thing. We are all so used to acting on the smallest hunger pangs that we forget what it's like to feel genuinely hungry. Learn to 'own' your hunger and take control of how you deal with it.
- Get moving. Increased activity will complement your weight loss efforts. Think about what you are doing each day: choose the stairs instead of the lift, walk to the shops instead of driving. Making small changes will not only help you burn calories but will make you feel healthier and more in control of your weight loss.

The Healthy

medic food for life

BREAKFAST
recipes

GARLIC & THYME TOMATOES

180 calories per serving

Ingredients

- 6 large beef tomatoes
- 2 tsp crushed garlic
- 1 tsp dried thyme
- 1 tbsp olive oil
- 75g/3oz sliced onions
- 1 small ciabatta roll
- Salt & pepper to taste

Method

1 Cut the tomatoes into quarters and slice the ciabatta roll open.

2 Mix together the garlic, thyme & olive oil and heat in a frying pan.

3 Season the tomatoes well and add to the frying pan along with the onions, gently sautéing until everything is soft and cooked through.

4 Meanwhile place the ciabatta halves in a toaster and lightly toast.

5 Tip the cooked tomatoes on the ciabatta halves. Season & serve.

CHEFS NOTE
You could use a little additional olive oil to drizzle onto the ciabatta loaves if you like.

CREAMY PAPRIKA MUSHROOMS ON TOAST

220 calories per serving

Ingredients

- 1 tbsp olive oil
- 2 tsp crushed garlic
- 250g/9oz sliced chestnut mushrooms
- 1 tsp paprika

- 60ml/¼ cup low fat crème fraiche
- 2 pieces wholemeal bread
- 2 tbsp freshly chopped flat leaf parsley
- Salt & pepper to taste

Method

1 Heat the oil in a frying pan and add the garlic.

2 Sauté gently for 1 minute before adding the mushrooms.

3 Continue cooking until the mushrooms are soft and cooked through, add the paprika and combine well.

4 Meanwhile place the bread in a toaster and lightly toast.

5 Stir the cream fraiche into the frying pan, warm for a minute and tip the creamy mushrooms onto the toast.

6 Sprinkle with chopped parsley, season and serve.

CHEFS NOTE

Any type of mushrooms will work well in this recipe.

MEXICAN SCRAMBLED EGGS

330 calories per serving

Ingredients

- 1 red or orange pepper
- 4 large free-range eggs
- 1 tsp low cal 'butter' spread
- ½ tsp each crushed chilli flakes & ground cumin

- 2 pieces wholemeal bread
- 2 tbsp freshly chopped flat leaf parsley
- Salt & pepper to taste

Method

1 De-seed and slice the pepper.

2 Break the eggs into a bowl. Lightly beat with a fork & season with a little salt & lots of black pepper.

3 Heat the 'butter' in a frying pan and add the peppers, gently sautéing until softened.

4 Stir through the chilli flakes & cumin and cook for a minute longer.

5 Meanwhile place the bread in a toaster and lightly toast.

6 Tip the eggs into the frying pan and move around the pan until the eggs begin to scramble. As soon as they begin to set divide over the toast.

7 Sprinkle with parsley and serve.

CHEFS NOTE

Don't cook the eggs for too long. Take off the heat the moment the eggs begin to set as the residual heat will keep on cooking the eggs whilst you serve them up.

EASY CHEESE & CHIVE OMELETTE

290 calories per serving

Ingredients

- 2 large free-range eggs
- 50g/2oz grated low fat cheddar cheese
- 2 tbsp freshly chopped chives
- 1 tsp olive oil
- 50g/2oz rocket leaves
- Salt & pepper to taste

Method

1 Break the eggs into a bowl, along with the cheese and chives. Lightly beat with a fork and season with a little salt & lots of black pepper.

2 Place the oil on a medium heat in a small frying pan.

3 When the oil is hot tip the omelette mixture into the pan, tilting the pan to ensure the mixture is evenly spread over the base of the pan.

4 When the eggs are set underneath, fold the omelette in half and continue to cook for 2 mins.

5 Check the eggs are set and serve with the rocket leaves sprinkled all over the top.

CHEFS NOTE

The eggs shouldn't take more than about 3-4 minutes to set so this is a really quick & tasty breakfast choice.

CORIANDER & LIME AVOCADO BREAKFAST

270 calories per serving

Ingredients

- 1 ripe avocado
- 100g/3½oz cherry tomatoes
- 50g/2oz chopped onion
- ½ tsp crushed chilli flakes
- 1 tbsp lime juice
- 3 tbsp freshly chopped coriander/cilantro
- 100g/3½oz spinach leaves
- 2 pieces wholemeal bread
- Salt & pepper to taste

Method

1 Skin, de-stone and cube the avocado. Roughly chop the cherry tomatoes.

2 Combine the avocado, tomatoes, onions, chilli, lime & coriander together. Season well and put to one side.

3 Place the bread in a toaster and lightly toast.

4 Meanwhile gently heat a saucepan and add the spinach leaves. Stir until the spinach begins to wilt.

5 Place the wilted spinach on the toast and divide the avocado mix over the top.

6 Check the seasoning & serve immediately.

CHEFS NOTE

The easiest way to deal with an avocado is to cut it in half (you'll need to work around the centre stone). When halved, dig the point of the knife into the stone to lever it out, then use a large spoon to scoop each half of the avocado out whole.

INDIAN SPICED BREAKFAST

360
calories per serving

Ingredients

- 200g/7oz miniature salad potatoes
- 4 large free range eggs
- 1 tbsp olive oil
- 75g/3oz chopped onion
- 75g/3oz fresh peas
- ½ tsp each turmeric, cumin & chilli flakes
- 1 tsp garam masala
- Salt & pepper to taste

Method

1 Chop the potatoes into quarters and place in salted boiling water. Boil for 5 minutes or until tender.

2 Meanwhile break the eggs into a bowl and lightly beat with a fork.

3 Heat the oil in a frying pan and gently sauté the onions until softened. Add the peas, turmeric, cumin, chilli flakes & garam masala.

4 When the potatoes are tender, drain and add to the frying pan. Combine well and tip in the eggs. Increase the heat and cook until the eggs are scrambled.

5 Check the seasoning & serve immediately.

CHEFS NOTE
If you don't have garam masala, cumin and turmeric feel free to just use a couple of teaspoons of curry powder to flavour this spicy morning dish.

19

SUNDRIED TOMATO FRITTATA

325 calories per serving

Ingredients

- 3 sundried tomatoes
- 5 free-range eggs
- 1 tbsp olive oil
- 125g/4oz chopped onion
- 125g/4oz fresh peas
- 2 tsp grated Parmesan cheese
- 2 tbsp freshly chopped basil or chives
- Salt & pepper to taste

Method

1 Finely chop the sundried tomatoes.

2 Break the eggs into a bowl and lightly beat with a fork.

3 Heat the oil in a frying pan and gently sauté the onions and peas for a few minutes until softened.

4 Mix the Parmesan into the eggs and tip this into the frying pan. Tilt the pan to ensure the mixture covers the bottom of the pan completely.

5 Place a cover the pan, reduce the heat and leave to cook for a few minutes. Flip the frittata over and cook the other side.

6 Cut into wedges and serve with the chopped basil or chives sprinkled over the top.

CHEFS NOTE
Sundried tomatoes are best bought in jars as they are already hydrated and don't need to be soaked in water.

DEVILLED CREAMY KIDNEYS

340 calories per serving

Ingredients

- 4 fresh lamb kidneys
- 1 tbsp olive oil
- 2 tsp crushed garlic
- 75g/3oz sliced mushrooms
- 75g/3oz chopped onion
- ½ tsp each paprika & crushed chilli flakes

- 1 tbsp Worcestershire sauce
- 2 pieces wholemeal bread
- 2 tbsp low fat crème fraiche
- 2 tbsp freshly chopped flat leaf parsley
- Salt & pepper to taste

Method

1 Halve and trim the lamb kidneys.

2 Heat the oil in a frying pan and gently sauté the garlic, mushrooms & onions for a few minutes until softened.

3 Add the kidneys, paprika, chilli & Worcestershire sauce to the pan. Combine well and cook the kidneys for aprox 4/5 minutes each side.

4 Meanwhile place the bread in a toaster and lightly toast.

5 When the kidneys are cooked through, stir in the crème fraiche and serve on toast with parsley sprinkled over the top.

CHEFS NOTE

Lamb kidneys are a nutritious economical ingredient, which are available at any supermarket meat counter.

PORTABELLA MUSHROOMS & SPINACH

210 calories per serving

Ingredients

- 1 tbsp olive oil
- 1 tsp crushed garlic
- 4 large portabella mushrooms
- 2 large free range eggs
- 200g/7oz spinach leaves
- 1 tsp low fat 'butter' spread
- Salt & pepper to taste

Method

1 Preheat the oven grill & boil a kettle of water.

2 Mix the oil and garlic together and brush over each mushroom. Season well and place under the grill for 2/3 minutes each side.

3 Meanwhile fill a frying pan with boiling water and break the eggs into the gently simmering pan. Leave to poach while the mushrooms cook and you get started on the spinach.

4 Add the spinach leaves to a saucepan with the 'butter' and keep on stirring until wilted.

5 Put the mushrooms on the plates. Arrange the spinach over the top and add a poached egg.

6 Serve with lots of black pepper.

CHEFS NOTE
This dish requires a little coordination but it's simple & tasty.

HOMEMADE MUESLI

360
calories per
serving

Ingredients

- 100g/3½oz rolled oats
- 2 tbsp sultanas
- 1 tbsp almond flakes
- 50g/2oz dried chopped apricots
- 250ml/1 cup pure apple juice

- 2 eating apples
- 2 tbsp fat free Greek yoghurt
- 1 banana
- 2 tbsp runny honey

Method

1 Combine together the oats, sultanas, almond flakes, apricots and apple juice. Mix well and put to one side to soak for 10 minutes.

2 Meanwhile peel and grate the apples. Peel & slice the banana.

3 After 10 minutes check the apple juice has soaked into the oats and fruit. Divide into two bowls and cover with the grated apple.

4 Dollop a tablespoon of Greek yoghurt on top and arrange the banana slices in a mound on the yoghurt.

5 Drizzle the honey over the top and serve immediately.

CHEFS NOTE
Add a little more yoghurt or a dash of semi skimmed milk if you feel the muesli needs it when serving.

The Healthy

medic food for life

LUNCH
recipes

SERVES 2

MEDITERRANEAN SPAGHETTI

350 calories per serving

Ingredients

- 200g/7oz cherry tomatoes
- 100g/3½oz pitted black olives
- 150g/5oz wholemeal spaghetti
- 1 tbsp olive oil

- 1 tsp crushed garlic
- 1 tsp crushed chilli flakes
- 4 tbsp freshly chopped basil
- Salt & pepper to taste

Method

1 First cut each of the cherry tomatoes & black olives in half.

2 Cook the spaghetti in a pan of salted boiling water until tender.

3 Meanwhile heat the olive oil in a high-sided frying pan and gently sauté the garlic, chilli, tomatoes and olives whilst the pasta cooks.

4 Drain the cooked pasta and add to the frying pan.

5 Toss well and sprinkle with the freshly chopped basil.

6 Season & serve.

CHEFS NOTE
This really simple pasta dish is a staple of southern Italy.

SALMON FILLET & SPRING GREENS

270 calories per serving

Ingredients

- 200g/7oz shredded spring greens
- 150g/5oz fresh peas
- 1 tbsp capers
- 1 tbsp fat free Greek yoghurt
- 1 tbsp horseradish sauce
- 1 tbsp lemon juice
- 250g/9oz cooked salmon fillet
- Salt & pepper to taste

Method

1 Plunge the spring greens and fresh peas into a pan of salted boiling water and cook for 2 minutes.

2 Rinse and chop the capers. Mix together the yoghurt, horseradish & lemon juice.

3 Flake the cooked salmon and gently combine with the caper mayonnaise.

4 Drain the greens and peas. Toss with the salmon and caper mayonnaise, divide onto plates and serve.

CHEFS NOTE

Feel free to use frozen peas if you don't have fresh peas but you'll need to cook them for longer.

CHICKEN & GORGONZOLA SALAD

395
calories per serving

Ingredients

- 250g/9oz cooked chicken breast
- 2 large plum tomatoes
- 50g/2oz Gorgonzola cheese
- 1 avocado
- 1 tbsp extra virgin olive oil
- 1 tbsp cider vinegar
- 1 tbsp fat free Greek yoghurt
- 2 tsp Dijon mustard
- 200g/7oz spinach leaves
- 2 tbsp freshly chopped basil
- Salt & pepper to taste

Method

1 Slice the chicken breast into strips.

2 Slice the tomatoes & crumble the cheese.

3 De-stone, peel & slice the avocado.

4 Mix together the olive oil, vinegar, yoghurt & mustard.

5 Toss everything, except the basil, together in a large bowl.

6 Divide onto plates, sprinkle with the chopped basil and serve.

CHEFS NOTE
Gorgonzola is a lovely rich cheese. Feel free to use whichever blue cheese you prefer.

SERVES 2

FRUITY CHICKEN COUSCOUS

395
calories per serving

Ingredients

- 2 tbsp sultanas
- 250g/9oz cooked chicken breast
- 125g/4oz chopped onions
- 1 tsp crushed garlic
- 1 tsp ground coriander/cilantro
- 1 tbsp lemon juice
- 180ml/¾ cup chicken stock
- 100g/3½oz wholemeal giant couscous
- Lemon wedges to serve
- 2 tbsp freshly chopped coriander/cilantro
- Salt & pepper to taste

Method

1 Roughly chop the sultanas & chicken breast.

2 Gently sauté the chopped onions, garlic, ground coriander & lemon juice for a few minutes. Then add the chicken to warm through for a minute or two.

3 Whilst the onions are cooking, place the couscous & sultanas is a pan with the hot stock. Bring the pan to the boil, remove from the heat cover and leave to stand for 3-4 minutes or until all the stock is absorbed and the couscous is tender.

4 Fluff the couscous with a fork and pile into the onion pan. Mix well, divide onto plates and serve with fresh lemon wedges on the side and chopped coriander sprinkled over the top.

CHEFS NOTE
Mint is also a good addition to this dish if you want to put your own twist on things.

29

OLIVE OIL & GARLIC LINGUINE

375
calories per serving

Ingredients

- 150g/5oz wholemeal linguine
- 2 tbsp extra virgin olive oil
- 2 tsp crushed garlic
- 125g/4oz sliced onions
- ½ tsp crushed chilli flakes
- 1 tbsp lemon juice
- 4 tbsp freshly chopped flat leaf parsley
- Salt & pepper to taste

Method

1 Cook the linguine in a pan of salted boiling water until tender.

2 Meanwhile gently heat the extra virgin olive oil in a high-sided frying pan and sauté the garlic, onions, chilli & lemon juice whilst the pasta cooks.

3 Drain the cooked pasta and add to the frying pan.

4 Toss well and sprinkle with the freshly chopped parsley.

5 Season & serve.

CHEFS NOTE
Good quality extra virgin olive all makes a real difference to the taste of this dish but regular olive oil will work fine if that's all you have.

SUGAR SNAP PEA & PRAWN STIR-FRY

390 calories per serving

Ingredients

- 1 tbsp olive oil
- 1 tsp crushed garlic
- 1 tsp chopped ginger
- 250g/9oz shelled king prawns
- 1 red pepper
- 3 tbsp soy sauce

- 150g/9oz trimmed sugar snap peas
- 250g/9oz ready-to-go microwaveable wholemeal rice
- 1 bunch spring onions/scallions
- Salt & pepper to taste

Method

1 Heat the olive oil in a frying pan or wok and gently sauté the garlic and ginger for a minute. Add the prawns and cook for a few minutes until they begin to pink up.

2 Meanwhile quickly de-seed & slice the red pepper. Add to the pan along with the sugar snap peas and soy sauce.

3 Stir-fry for 3-4 minutes whilst you microwave the rice.

4 Check the prawns are cooked through and when the rice is ready add to the pan. Combine for a minute or two.

5 Slice the spring onions and use these as a fresh garnish while you plate up your prawn stir-fry.

CHEFS NOTE

You could use mange tout or fresh peas in place of sugar snap peas if you prefer.

BROCCOLI & ANCHOVY STIR-FRY

325 calories per serving

Ingredients

- 6 tinned anchovy fillets
- 250g/9oz purple sprouting broccoli
- 1 tbsp olive oil
- 2 tsp crushed garlic
- 125g/4oz chopped red onion

- 1 tsp crushed chilli flakes
- 250g/9oz ready-to-go microwaveable wholemeal rice
- Salt & pepper to taste

Method

1 Drain the anchovy fillets & roughly chop the broccoli.

2 Heat the olive oil in a frying pan or wok and gently sauté the garlic and red onion for 2 minutes. Add the anchovy fillets and cook for a further 2 mins until they begin to break up.

3 Add the chopped broccoli to the pan along with the crushed chilli flakes.

4 Stir-fry for 5-6 minutes whilst you microwave the rice.

5 When the rice is ready, check the broccoli is cooked to your liking, and add the rice to the pan.

6 Combine for a minute or two, check the seasoning and serve.

CHEFS NOTE
Purple sprouting broccoli is a lovely seasonal vegetable which is very tender and cooks in minutes. Any young tender stem broccoli will do the job for this recipe.

FRESH CORIANDER PRAWNS & RICE

340 calories per serving

Ingredients

- 1 tbsp olive oil
- 1 tsp crushed garlic
- 250g/9oz shelled king prawns
- 1 tbsp soy sauce
- 250g/9oz ready-to-go microwaveable wholemeal rice
- 1 tbsp Thai fish sauce
- 4 tbsp freshly chopped coriander/cilantro
- ½ tsp crushed chilli flakes
- 1 bunch spring onions/scallions
- Salt & pepper to taste

Method

1 Heat the olive oil in a frying pan or wok and gently sauté the garlic for a minute.

2 Add the prawns, soy sauce & fish sauce and cook until the prawns begin to pink up. Meanwhile microwave the rice.

3 Check the prawns are cooked through, add the chopped coriander, chilli flakes and rice to the pan. Combine for a minute or two.

4 Slice the spring onions and toss through the rice. Season & serve.

CHEFS NOTE

Having fresh herbs such as coriander/basil or parsley growing on a window ledge is really useful when you are putting together quick & easy meals.

CHINESE ASPARAGUS & PRAWN LUNCH

310 calories per serving

Ingredients

- 200g/14oz asparagus tips
- 1 tbsp olive oil
- 1 tsp crushed garlic
- 1 tsp chopped ginger
- 250g/9oz shelled king prawns
- 1 tbsp soy sauce

- 1 tsp Chinese five spice powder
- ½ tsp crushed chilli flakes
- 250g/9oz ready-to-go microwaveable wholemeal rice
- 125g/4oz rocket leaves
- Salt & pepper to taste

Method

1 Roughly chop the asparagus tips.

2 Heat the olive oil in a frying pan or wok and gently sauté the garlic & ginger for a minute.

3 Add the prawns, asparagus, soy sauce, Chinese five spice powder and chilli flakes.

4 Cook until the prawns are pink and the asparagus is tender. Meanwhile microwave the rice.

5 Check the prawns are cooked through. Add the rice to the pan and combine for a minute or two.

6 Quickly toss through the rocket. Season and serve immediately.

CHEFS NOTE
You could try substituting spinach for rocket if you like. Add the spinach at the same time as the asparagus so that it has time to wilt.

STEAK & STILTON SALAD

420 calories per serving

Ingredients

- 250g/9oz sirloin steak
- 2 tbsp olive oil
- ½ tsp paprika
- 1 red pepper
- 200g/7oz cherry tomatoes

- 2 romaine lettuces
- 1 tsp crushed garlic
- 50g/2oz stilton cheese
- Salt & pepper to taste

Method

1 Trim any fat off the steak. Lightly brush with a little of the olive oil & the paprika. Season and put a frying pan on a high heat.

2 While the pan is heating up de-seed and slice the red pepper. Halve the tomatoes & shred the lettuce.

3 Place the steak in the smoking hot dry pan and cook for 1-2 minutes each side, or to your liking. When the steak is cooked put to one side to rest.

4 Mix the garlic with the rest of the olive oil and toss in a large bowl with the peppers, tomatoes, & lettuce. Crumble the stilton cheese and combine on plates with the rest of the salad.

5 Slice the rested steak very thinly and place on top. Season and serve.

CHEFS NOTE
Stilton cheese and steak are a great combination. You could melt a little of the cheese on top of the steak whilst it's cooking if you like.

35

FRESH BALSAMIC TUNA SALAD

275 calories per serving

Ingredients

- 250g/9oz fresh tuna steak
- 2 tbsp olive oil
- 3 tbsp balsamic vinegar

- 1 baby gem lettuce
- 200g/7oz watercress
- Salt & pepper to taste

Method

1 Season the tuna and put a frying pan on a high heat with the olive oil and balsamic vinegar.

2 While the pan is heating up shred the baby gem lettuce and toss with the watercress.

3 Place the tuna in the pan and cook for 2 minutes each side. Remove the tuna from the pan and, using two forks, separate the tuna steak into strips.

4 Place the tuna strips on top of the watercress and drizzle any pan juices over the salad.

CHEFS NOTE

Add a little more balsamic vinegar and olive oil to dress the tuna if you like.

BALSAMIC VINEGAR & SUNDRIED TOMATO SPAGHETTI

330 calories per serving

Ingredients

- 150g/5oz wholemeal spaghetti
- 1 tbsp olive oil
- 125g/4oz sliced onions
- 2 tbsp sundried tomato puree/paste
- 2 tbsp balsamic vinegar
- 2 tbsp freshly chopped oregano
- Salt & pepper to taste

Method

1 Cook the spaghetti in a pan of salted boiling water until tender.

2 Meanwhile heat the olive oil in a high-sided frying pan and gently sauté the onions, sundried tomato puree & balsamic vinegar whilst the pasta cooks.

3 Drain the cooked pasta and add to the frying pan.

4 Toss well and sprinkle with freshly chopped oregano. Season & serve.

CHEFS NOTE
You could use chopped sundried tomatoes out of jar rather than paste.

ANCHOVY & FRESH CHILLI LINGUINE

360
calories per serving

Ingredients

- 150g/5oz wholemeal linguine
- 1 red chilli
- 1 tbsp olive oil
- 2 tsp crushed garlic

- 10 tinned anchovy fillets
- 2 tbsp lemon juice
- ½ tsp dried thyme
- Salt & pepper to taste

Method

1 Cook the spaghetti in a pan of salted boiling water until tender.

2 Meanwhile de-seed and finely chop the red chilli. Drain the anchovy fillets.

3 Heat the olive oil in a high-sided frying pan and gently sauté the garlic, anchovy fillets, lemon juice & dried thyme whilst the pasta cooks.

4 Drain the cooked pasta and add to the frying pan.

5 Toss well. Season & serve.

CHEFS NOTE
The anchovy fillets will dissolve to make a delicious salty base for this lovely dish.

PRAWN & LEMON ANGEL HAIR PASTA

385
calories per serving

Ingredients

- 150g/5oz wholemeal angel hair pasta
- ½ tsp dried chilli flakes
- 1 tbsp olive oil
- 1 tsp crushed garlic
- 250g/9oz shelled king prawns
- 2 tbsp lemon juice
- 4 tsp freshly chopped flat leaf parsley
- 1 lemon cut into wedges
- Salt & pepper to taste

Method

1 Cook the spaghetti in a pan of salted boiling water until tender.

2 Heat the olive oil in a high-sided frying pan and gently sauté the garlic, prawns & lemon juice whilst the pasta cooks.

3 When the prawns are pink and cooked through, drain the cooked pasta and add to the frying pan.

4 Toss well. Sprinkle with chopped parsley and serve with lemon wedges.

CHEFS NOTE
Angel hair pasta is a very thin spaghetti pasta which gives a light and delicate feel to the dish. Serve with lots of black pepper.

SOLE, LIME & SALSA

300
calories per
serving

Ingredients

- 1 tsp crushed garlic
- 1 tbsp olive oil
- 2 boneless, skinless sole fillets (approx. 125g/4oz each)
- 4 large plum tomatoes
- 75g/3oz chopped onion

- 1 avocado
- 2 tbsp freshly chopped coriander/cilantro
- 2 tbsp lime juice
- Lime juice/wedges to serve
- Salt & pepper to taste

Method

1 Mix together the garlic & olive oil and brush onto the sole fillets.

2 Heat a frying pan and gently begin to fry the fish (add a little more oil if needed).

3 Cook the sole for 2-3 minutes each side.

4 Meanwhile halve, de-stone, peel and cube the avocado.

5 Roughly chop the tomatoes and combine with the avocado, onions, chopped coriander and lime juice to make a salsa.

6 Season and serve the cooked lemon sole with the salsa and lime wedges.

CHEFS NOTE

Sole is a lovely delicate fish. Be careful not to overcook - when it flakes easily it's ready!

PAN FRIED COD & TOMATO SAUCE

270
calories per serving

Ingredients

- 2 boneless, skinless cod fillets (approx. 125g/4oz each)
- 1 tbsp olive oil
- 1 tsp crushed garlic
- 1 tbsp lemon juice

- 250ml/1 cup tomato passata/sieved tomatoes
- 1 tsp each sea salt & brown sugar
- 150g/5oz green beans
- Salt & pepper to taste

Method

1 Season the cod fillets and gently sauté the garlic in the olive oil for a few minutes.

2 Place the passata, salt & sugar in a saucepan and gently warm through, stirring occasional until it is piping hot.

3 Place the green beans in a steamer and steam for 5-8 minutes or until tender.

4 Meanwhile begin frying the cod fillets in the garlic and oil. Cook for 3-5 minutes each side depending on the thickness of the fillet.

5 Serve the cod fillets on a bed of green beans with the fresh tomato sauce poured over the top.

CHEFS NOTE
The sugar and salt will help balance the acidity of the tomato passata. Adjust to suit to your own taste.

SWEET CARROT SOUP

Ingredients

- 125g/4oz potatoes
- 300g/11oz carrot
- 1 tbsp olive oil
- 75g/3oz chopped onions

- 1lt/4 cups vegetable stock/broth
- 1 tsp runny honey
- Salt & pepper to taste

Method

1 Quickly chop up the potatoes & carrots (no need to peel).

2 Heat the oil in a saucepan and add the onions, potatoes and carrots. Sauté for a minute or two and add the stock.

3 Turn up the heat, bring to the boil and simmer for 7-10 minutes or until all the vegetables are soft.

4 Add the honey and stir well.

5 Blend to a smooth consistency, check the seasoning and serve.

CHEFS NOTE

Soups are a great simple lunch. You can store in the fridge to reheat when you need.

FRESH MACKEREL & MUSTARD DRESSING

370 calories per serving

Ingredients

- 2 fresh, boned headless mackerel (approx. 150g/5oz each)
- 50g/2oz low fat 'butter' spread
- 1 tbsp wholegrain mustard
- 1 tbsp lemon juice
- 150g/5oz shredded spring greens
- 2 tbsp freshly chopped chives
- Salt & pepper to taste

Method

1 Preheat the grill and season the fish.

2 Gently heat the butter, mustard & lemon juice in a pan. Remove from the heat and brush a little onto both sides of the mackerel.

3 Place the mackerel under the grill and cook for approx. 5 minutes each side or until the fish is cooked through.

4 Whilst the fish is cooking, steam or boil the spring greens until tender. Drain, return to the pan and use the rest of the butter & mustard dressing to coat the greens in the saucepan.

5 Serve the cooked fish on top of the mustard greens sprinkled with chives.

CHEFS NOTE

It's best to 'butterfly' (open up) the fish to speed up the cooking time.

CURRIED CAULIFLOWER SOUP

240
calories per serving

Ingredients

- 200g/7oz cauliflower florets
- 125g/4oz potatoes
- 1 tbsp olive oil
- 75g/3oz chopped onions
- 750ml/3 cups vegetable stock/broth
- 1 tbsp medium curry powder
- 250ml/1 cup semi skimmed milk
- Salt & pepper to taste

Method

1 Quickly chop up the cauliflower & potatoes (no need to peel).

2 Heat the oil in a saucepan and add the onions. Sauté for a minute or two and add the stock, cauliflower, potatoes & curry powder.

3 Turn up the heat, bring to the boil and simmer for 7-10 minutes or until all the vegetables are soft.

4 Add the milk, stir well and heat through for a minute.

5 Blend to a smooth consistency, check the seasoning and serve.

CHEFS NOTE
The milk gives the soup a creamy texture but you can substitute for stock if you prefer.

HOT CHILLI PRAWNS

340 calories per serving

Ingredients

- 1 red pepper
- 300g/11oz shelled king prawns
- 75g/3oz sliced onions
- 2 tsp crushed garlic
- 1 tsp sliced ginger
- 1 tbsp olive oil
- 1 tbsp lime juice

- 1 tsp each paprika, coriander/cilantro & crushed chilli flakes
- 250g/9oz ready-to-go microwaveable wholemeal rice
- 2 tbsp freshly chopped coriander/cilantro
- Lime wedges to serve
- Salt & pepper to taste

Method

1 De-seed and slice the red pepper. Season the prawns.

2 Gently sauté the sliced peppers, onions, garlic & ginger in the olive oil for a few minutes until softened.

3 Add the prawns, dried spices & lime juice and cook for 5-8 minutes or until the prawns are pink and cooked through.

4 Whilst the prawns are cooking microwave the rice.

5 When both the prawns and rice are ready tip the prawns and juices onto the top of the rice.

6 Sprinkle with chopped coriander and serve with lime wedges.

CHEFS NOTE
This is a really simple meal. Add more or less chilli flakes to suit your own taste.

PESTO CRUSTED SALMON

375 calories per serving

Ingredients

- 250g/9oz sweet potatoes
- 2 boneless, skinless salmon fillets (approx. 125g/4oz each)
- 1 tbsp green pesto
- 1 tbsp fresh breadcrumbs
- 125g/4oz sugar snap peas
- Lemon wedges to serve
- Salt & pepper to taste

Method

1 Preheat the grill and put a kettle on to boil.

2 Peel & dice the sweet potatoes and place in a saucepan of boiling water.

3 Mix the pesto and breadcrumbs together and smother on top of the salmon fillets. Place under the grill and cook for 10-13 minutes or until the salmon fillets are cooked through.

4 Whilst the salmon is cooking steam the sugar snap peas.

5 Drain the sweet potatoes and serve with the sugar snap peas & salmon with lemon wedges on the side.

CHEFS NOTE

Fresh breadcrumbs are really easy to make: place a slice of bread in the food processor and pulse for a few seconds. Simple!

THYME & MUSHROOM SOUP

180 calories per serving

Ingredients

- 125g/4oz potatoes
- 1 tbsp olive oil
- 300g/11oz sliced mushrooms
- 75g/3oz chopped onions
- 1 tsp dried thyme
- 750ml/3 cups vegetable stock/broth
- 250ml/1 cup semi skimmed milk
- Salt & pepper to taste

Method

1 Quickly chop up the potatoes (no need to peel).

2 Heat the oil in a saucepan and add the sliced mushrooms, onions & thyme. Sauté for a few minutes and then add the stock.

3 Turn up the heat, bring to the boil and simmer for 7-10 minutes or until all the vegetables are soft.

4 Add the milk, stir well and heat through for a minute.

5 Blend to a smooth consistency, check the seasoning and serve.

CHEFS NOTE
A swirl of single cream and chopped chives makes a nice serving addition to this simple soup.

SHREDDED CHICKEN & LEEK SOUP

230 calories per serving

Ingredients

- 125g/4oz potatoes
- 2 leeks
- 125g/4oz cooked chicken breast
- 1 tbsp olive oil
- 1 tsp dried mixed herbs
- 1lt/4 cups chicken stock/broth
- Salt & pepper to taste

Method

1 Quickly chop up the potatoes (no need to peel), slice the leeks and shred the chicken with two forks.

2 Heat the oil in a saucepan and add the leeks, potatoes & mixed herbs. Sauté for a few minutes and then add the stock.

3 Turn up the heat, bring to the boil and simmer for 7-10 minutes or until all the vegetables are soft.

4 Blend to a smooth consistency and return to the pan.

5 Add the shredded chicken and heat through for a minute or two.

6 Check the seasoning and serve.

CHEFS NOTE

This soup has a nice meaty texture but you could add the chicken before blending if you prefer.

ASPARAGUS & PARMESAN SOUP

310 calories per serving

Ingredients

- 125g/4oz potatoes
- 1 tbsp olive oil
- 1 tsp crushed garlic
- 75g/3oz chopped onions
- 750ml/3 cups vegetable stock/broth
- 200g/7oz asparagus tips
- 250ml/1 cup dry white wine
- 125g/4oz straight-to-wok wholemeal noodles
- 2 tsp grated Parmesan
- Salt & pepper to taste

Method

1 Quickly chop up the potatoes (no need to peel).

2 Heat the oil in a saucepan and add the potatoes, garlic & onions. Sauté for a few minutes and then add the stock.

3 Turn up the heat, bring to the boil and simmer for 5 minutes. Add the asparagus tips, wine and noodles and cook for a further 3-4 minutes or until all the vegetables are tender.

4 Roughly blend the soup with just a couple of pulses in the food processor. This soup is best left with a chunky texture.

5 Check the seasoning, sprinkle with Parmesan and serve.

CHEFS NOTE
Add some spring onion ribbons to garnish if you like: to make these just cut the spring onions very finely lengthways and separate into ribbons.

GARLIC GNOCCHI & ROCKET

370
calories per serving

Ingredients

- 350g/11oz gnocchi
- 2 tbsp olive oil
- 2 tsp crushed garlic

- 125g/4oz rocket
- 125g/4oz cherry tomatoes
- Salt & pepper to taste

Method

1 Place the gnocchi in a pan of salted boiling water.

2 Cook for 2-3 minutes or until the gnocchi begins to float to the top.

3 Meanwhile gently heat the olive oil in a saucepan and sauté the garlic.

4 Halve the cherry tomatoes and add to the saucepan.

5 As soon as the gnocchi is cooked, drain and place in the frying pan with the olive oil and garlic.

6 Move the gnocchi around for a minute or two to coat each dumpling in the garlic oil.

7 Add the rocket to the pan, quickly toss and serve.

CHEFS NOTE
Don't over cook the gnocchi. As soon as the dumplings begin to float to the top remove from the heat and drain.

TENDERSTEM BROCCOLI PENNE

380
calories per serving

Ingredients

- 200g/7oz tenderstem broccoli
- 150g/5oz dried penne
- 1 tbsp olive oil
- 3 tsp crushed garlic

- 2 tsp crushed chilli flakes
- 6 tinned anchovy fillets
- Salt & pepper to taste

Method

1 Boil a kettle of water.

2 Finely chop the tenderstem broccoli, discarding any thick woody ends & drain the anchovy fillets.

3 Cook the penne in a pan of salted boiling water until tender.

4 Meanwhile gently heat the olive oil, garlic, chilli & anchovy fillets in a high-sided frying pan and sauté whilst the pasta cooks.

5 Drain the cooked penne and add to the pan.

6 Toss well, season & serve.

CHEFS NOTE
Tenderstem broccoli or purple sprouting broccoli is much easier to handle for quick meals than the large traditional broccoli 'heads'.

CANNELLINI BEAN & TUNA SALAD

380
calories per serving

Ingredients

- 125g/4oz cherry tomatoes
- 200g/7oz tinned cannellini beans
- 125g/4oz asparagus tips
- 200g/7oz no drain tinned tuna
- 125g/4oz sliced red onions

- 2 tbsp olive oil
- 1 tsp each crushed garlic, lemon juice & Dijon mustard
- Salt & pepper to taste

Method

1 Boil a kettle of water.

2 Slice the tomatoes in half. Drain the cannellini beans, rinse with cold water and put to one side.

3 Pour the boiling water into a saucepan on place on a high heat. Add the asparagus tips and cook for 3-4 minutes. Take off the heat, rinse with cold water and leave to cool.

4 Meanwhile mix together the tomatoes, beans, tuna, onions, oil, garlic, lemon juice & mustard together in a large bowl.

5 Divide onto two plates. Place the asparagus tips on top and serve.

CHEFS NOTE
You could use flageolet or chickpeas for this recipe if you prefer.

FRESH PRAWN & LEMON MAYO SALAD

320 calories per serving

Ingredients

- 2 baby gem lettuces
- 1 carrot
- ½ cucumber
- 2 tsp capers
- 1 tbsp low fat mayonnaise

- 2 tbsp lemon juice
- 3 tbsp extra virgin olive oil
- 2 tbsp freshly chopped flat leaf parsley.
- 300g/11oz fresh, cooked prawns
- Salt & pepper to taste

Method

1 Shred the baby gem lettuces.

2 Use a potato peeler to peel the carrot and cucumber. Discard the peelings and then use the peeler to make thin ribbons out of the carrot and cucumber flesh (discard the soft core of the cucumber).

3 Mix the carrot & cucumber ribbons with the shredded lettuce and arrange onto plates.

4 Rinse and chop the capers. Combine with the mayonnaise, lemon juice, olive oil, parsley & prawns.

5 Pile the mayonnaise prawns on top of the salad. Check the seasoning and serve.

CHEFS NOTE
You could also serve with fresh lemon wedges if you have them to hand.

PANCETTA & SPROUT SALAD

240
calories per serving

Ingredients

- 250g/12oz prepared Brussels sprouts
- 1 tbsp olive oil
- 125g/4oz sliced mushrooms
- 50g/2oz pancetta cubes
- 1 tbsp crème fraiche
- Salt & pepper to taste

Method

1 Slice the sprouts thinly so they fall into shreds.

2 Heat the olive oil in a frying pan and add the pancetta & sliced mushrooms. Cook for 3-4 minutes before adding the sprouts.

3 Sauté for about 6 minutes or until the sprouts are softened. Season with lots of black pepper.

4 Stir through the creme fraiche and serve.

CHEFS NOTE
Bacon and sprouts are a classic combination. Make sure you shred your sprouts well so that they cook quickly.

MEXICAN CHICKEN RICE

410
calories per
serving

Ingredients

- 200g/7oz cooked chicken breast
- 1 tbsp olive oil
- 1 tsp crushed garlic
- 75g/3oz chopped onions
- 250g/9oz ready-to-go microwaveable rice

- 1 tsp paprika
- ½ tsp crushed chilli flakes
- 200g/7oz tinned chopped tomatoes
- 150g/9oz peas
- Salt & pepper to taste

Method

1 Finely chop the cooked chicken.

2 Heat the olive oil in a frying pan and gently sauté the garlic & onions for a few minutes until softened.

3 Meanwhile microwave the rice and, when it's ready, add to the pan along with the paprika, chilli flakes, chopped tomatoes & peas.

4 Simmer on the hob until everything is piping hot.

5 Season well and serve.

CHEFS NOTE
Simmer on quite a high heat so that the juice from the tinned tomatoes reduces a little.

The Healthy

medic food for life

DINNER
recipes

STEAK WITH SWEET POTATOES & CREAMED SPINACH

440
calories per serving

Ingredients

- 250g/9oz sirloin steak
- 1 tsp olive oil
- 300g/11oz sweet potatoes
- 125g/4oz spinach leaves
- 1 tbsp fresh single cream
- 1 tsp grated Parmesan
- Salt & pepper to taste

Method

1 Boil a kettle of water and use the water to fill a saucepan on the hob.

2 Peel the sweet potatoes, cut into 1cm slices and cook in the saucepan for 10-12 minutes or until they are tender.

3 Meanwhile trim any fat off the steak. Season and brush with the olive oil, while you put a frying pan on a high heat. Place the steak in the smoking-hot dry pan and cook for 1-2 minutes each side, or to your liking.

4 When the steak is cooked, put to one side to rest for 3 minutes then slice into thin strips.

5 Whilst the steak is resting place the spinach in a clean saucepan and wilt for a minute or two on a medium heat stirring constantly. Add the cream & Parmesan and combine.

6 Serve the steak with the creamed spinach and sweet potatoes on the side.

CHEFS NOTE
Don't let the spinach wilt too much, it's best to come off the heat when it's reduced in size by about half.

ASPARAGUS & CHICKEN SINGLE PAN SUPPER

430 calories per serving

Ingredients

- 200g/7oz asparagus tips
- 250g/9oz cooked chicken breast
- 1 tbsp olive oil
- 75g/3oz sliced onions
- 1 tsp crushed garlic
- 150g/5oz carrot batons

- 120ml/½ cup chicken stock
- ½ tsp dried thyme
- 250g/9oz ready-to-go microwaveable wholemeal rice
- Salt & pepper to taste

Method

1 Roughly chop the asparagus tips & slice the chicken into strips.

2 Heat the oil in a frying pan and gently sauté the onion, garlic, carrot batons and asparagus tips for a few minutes until softened.

3 Add the chicken, stock & thyme to the pan. Increase the heat and cover.

4 Cook for 5-7 minutes or until the chicken is piping hot, the stock has reduced and the vegetables are tender.

5 Meanwhile microwave the rice and when everything else is ready tip the rice into the pan.

6 Remove from the heat, stir well and serve.

CHEFS NOTE
This is a lovely simple supper, which will keep the washing up to a minimum!

KALE, RICE & CHICKEN

420
calories per
serving

Ingredients

- 1 tbsp olive oil
- 125g/4oz sliced onion
- 2 tsp crushed garlic
- 250g/9oz cooked chicken breast
- 200g/7oz shredded kale
- 250ml/1 cup chicken stock
- ½ tsp crushed chilli flakes
- 250g/9oz ready-to-go microwaveable wholemeal rice
- 1 tbsp lemon juice
- Salt & pepper to taste

Method

1 Heat the oil in a frying pan and gently sauté the onions & garlic for a few minutes until softened.

2 Meanwhile shred the chicken into small strips using two forks.

3 Add the kale, stock & chilli to the pan and cook on a high heat until the stock has reduced and the kale is tender.

4 Add the shredded chicken and cook for a couple of minutes until the chicken is heated through.

5 Meanwhile microwave the rice and when everything else is ready tip the rice into the pan along with the lemon juice.

6 Remove from the heat, stir well, season & serve.

CHEFS NOTE
Discard any thick kale stems as these are tough and won't cook in the short time you have the pan on the hob.

CHICKEN KEBABS & COUSCOUS

390 calories per serving

Ingredients

- 250g/9oz raw, skinless chicken breast
- 3 tbsp fat free Greek yoghurt
- 1 tsp ground coriander/cilantro
- 1 tbsp lemon juice
- 1 tsp crushed garlic
- 180ml/¾ cup chicken stock
- 100g/3½oz giant wholemeal couscous
- 2 tbsp freshly chopped coriander/cilantro
- 4 kebab sticks
- Lemon wedges to serve
- Salt & pepper to taste

Method

1 Pre heat the grill & cube the chicken breast.

2 Mix together the yoghurt, ground coriander, lemon juice & garlic. Add the cubed chicken meat and combine well.

3 Place the chicken on the skewers, put under the grill and cook for 10-13 minutes or until it is cooked through.

4 Whilst the chicken is cooking, place the couscous in a pan with the hot stock. Bring the pan to the boil, remove from the heat, cover and leave to stand for 3-4 minutes or until all the stock is absorbed and the couscous is tender.

5 Fluff the couscous with a fork, divide onto plates and serve with the chicken kebabs on top, fresh lemon wedges on the side and coriander sprinkled over everything.

CHEFS NOTE
This is a North African inspired dish. Feel free to add a little chilli if you like.

BEEF KHEEMA

440
calories per
serving

Ingredients

- 1 tbsp olive oil
- 125g/4oz sliced onions
- 2 tsp crushed garlic
- 200g/7oz lean beef mince
- 60ml/¼ cup beef stock

- 1 tbsp curry powder
- 125g/4oz frozen peas
- 250g/9oz ready-to-go microwaveable wholemeal rice
- Salt & pepper to taste

Method

1 Heat the oil in a frying pan and gently sauté the onions & garlic for a few minutes until softened.

2 Add the mince to the pan. Increase the heat and brown for 2-3 minutes.

3 Keep the heat up and add the stock, curry powder & peas. Stir well and continue to cook for 6-8 minutes or until the mince is cooked through and the peas are tender.

4 Meanwhile cook the rice in the microwave.

5 Season well and serve the beef kheema piled on top of the rice.

CHEFS NOTE
Kheema should be a fairly dry mince dish, however feel free to add a little more stock if you feel it needs it during cooking.

MINTED CHICKEN COUSCOUS

390
calories per serving

Ingredients

- 250g/9oz cooked chicken breast
- 1 tsp crushed garlic
- 75g/3oz sliced onions
- 1 tbsp olive
- 180ml/¾ cup chicken stock

- 100g/3½oz couscous
- 2 tbsp lemon juice
- 3 tbsp freshly chopped mint
- Lemon wedges to serve
- Salt & pepper to taste

Method

1 Season and thinly slice the chicken breast into strips.

2 Gently sauté the garlic and onions in the olive oil for a few minutes until softened. Add the chicken to the pan to heat through.

3 Whilst the chicken is cooking place the couscous in a saucepan with the hot stock. Bring the pan to the boil, remove from the heat, cover and leave to stand for 3-4 minutes or until all the stock is absorbed and the couscous is tender.

4 Fluff the couscous with a fork and add to the frying pan along with the lemon juice and chopped mint.

5 Toss really well and serve immediately with lemon wedges.

CHEFS NOTE
Mint is a natural companion to this couscous dish but you could also try this recipe using fresh basil instead.

PAPRIKA STEAK WITH WARM POTATO SALAD

495 calories per serving

Ingredients

- 300g/11oz mini salad potatoes
- 1 bunch spring onions/scallions
- 225g/8oz sirloin steak
- 2 tsp paprika
- 1 tsp olive oil
- 1 tsp low fat mayonnaise
- 1 tsp Dijon mustard
- 100g/3½oz watercress
- Salt & pepper to taste

Method

1 Boil a kettle and use the water to fill a saucepan on the hob. Place the potatoes into the saucepan and cook for 6-8 minutes or until tender.

2 Meanwhile finely chop the spring onions. Trim any fat off the steak. Brush the paprika over both sides of the steak and season while you heat the oil in a frying pan on a high heat.

3 Place the steak in the smoking-hot pan and cook for 1-2 minutes each side, or to your liking. When the steak is cooked, put to one side to rest for 3 minutes then slice into thin strips.

4 Drain the potatoes and place in a bowl with the mayonnaise, mustard and chopped spring onions. Season and combine well to make a simple warm potato salad.

5 Serve the steak strips with the potato salad and watercress on the side.

CHEFS NOTE
If the salad potatoes are not very small halve them so that they will cook more quickly.

OYSTER SAUCE BEEF & RICE

430 calories per serving

Ingredients

- 1 red pepper
- Bunch spring onions/ scallions
- 250g/9oz sirloin steak
- 1 tbsp olive oil
- 150g/5oz chopped onion

- 3 tbsp oyster sauce
- 125g/4oz spinach leaves
- 250g/9oz ready-to-go microwaveable rice
- Salt & pepper to taste

Method

1 De-seed & slice the red pepper. Chop the spring onions, trim the steak of any fat & slice into strips.

2 Heat the olive oil in a frying pan or wok and gently sauté the chopped onion & sliced peppers for a few minutes until softened.

3 Add the oyster sauce and continue to cook whilst you microwave the rice.

4 Add the steak & spinach leaves to the pan and fry on a high heat for 1-2 minutes or until the steak is cooked to your liking and the spinach begins to wilt.

5 Add the rice to the pan. Remove from the heat and toss together with the chopped spring onions

6 Season and serve immediately.

CHEFS NOTE
Cook the steak to your liking. 1-2 minutes should leave it medium. Cook for longer if you like.

SIMPLE THAI CHICKEN NOODLES

405
calories per serving

Ingredients

- 200g/7oz cooked chicken breast
- 1 tbsp fish sauce
- 1 tbsp lime juice
- 4 tbsp soy sauce
- 1 tsp brown sugar
- 1 tbsp olive oil
- 75g/3oz chopped red onion

- 125g/4oz beansprouts
- 300g/11oz straight-to-wok wholemeal egg noodles
- ½ tsp crushed chilli flakes
- 4 tbsp freshly chopped coriander/cilantro
- Salt & pepper to taste

Method

1 Slice the cooked chicken breast into strips.

2 Mix together the fish sauce, lime juice, soy sauce & sugar together to make a simple Thai sauce. Check the balance and alter to suit your taste.

3 Heat the olive oil in a frying pan or wok and gently sauté the red onion for a few minutes until softened.

4 Add the sliced chicken, beansprouts, noodles, Thai sauce & chilli flakes and continue to cook until the dish is piping hot.

5 Divide into shallow bowls. Sprinkle with chopped coriander, season & serve.

CHEFS NOTE
You could also use chopped flat leaf parsley and/or mint as a garnish for this dish.

FRESH PEA & MINT CHICKEN

430
calories per serving

Ingredients

- 200g/7oz cooked chicken breast
- 1 tbsp olive oil
- 1 tbsp lemon juice
- 200g/7oz fresh peas
- 300g/11oz straight-to-wok wholemeal egg noodles
- 125g/4oz beansprouts
- 60ml/¼ cup chicken stock
- 4 tbsp freshly chopped mint
- 1 tbsp freshly grated Parmesan cheese
- Salt & pepper to taste

Method

1 Slice the cooked chicken breast into strips.

2 Heat the olive oil in a frying pan and add the chicken, lemon juice & fresh peas and cook for a few minutes.

3 Add the beansprouts, noodles & stock and cook until the dish is piping hot.

4 Add the chopped mint & stir through.

5 Divide into shallow bowls. Sprinkle with Parmesan, season & serve.

CHEFS NOTE
You could also make this dish using scallops or prawns rather than chicken if you wish.

SERVES 2

SWEET & SOUR CHICKEN & PEPPERS

420 calories per serving

Ingredients

- 2 red or yellow peppers
- 200g/7oz cooked chicken breast
- 1 tbsp olive oil
- 125g/4oz carrot batons
- 75g/3oz chopped onion
- 125g/4oz beansprouts
- 4 tbsp sweet & sour sauce
- 300g/11oz straight-to-wok wholemeal egg noodles
- 1 tbsp freshly chopped flat leaf parsley
- Salt & pepper to taste

Method

1 First de-seed and slice the peppers. Cut the cooked chicken breast into strips.

2 Heat the olive oil in a frying pan or wok and gently sauté the carrot batons, onions and sliced peppers for a few minutes until softened.

3 Add the sliced chicken, beansprouts, sweet & sour sauce & noodles and continue to cook until the dish is piping hot.

4 Divide into shallow bowls. Sprinkle with chopped parsley & serve.

CHEFS NOTE
This is a quick 'cheats' meal made with shop-bought sweet & sour sauce.

CHORIZO & PAPRIKA CHICKEN STIR-FRY

410 calories per serving

Ingredients

- 200g/7oz cooked chicken breast
- 125g/4oz chorizo
- 1 tbsp olive oil
- 150g/5oz chopped onions
- 1 tsp crushed garlic
- 1 tsp smoked paprika
- 125g/4oz spinach leaves
- 60ml/¼ cup chicken stock
- 250g/9oz ready-to-go microwaveable wholemeal rice
- Salt & pepper to taste

Method

1 Slice the chicken breast into strips and chop the chorizo.

2 Heat the olive oil in a frying pan or wok and gently sauté the chopped onion & garlic for a few minutes until softened.

3 Add the chicken, chorizo & paprika and continue to cook whilst you microwave the rice.

4 Add the spinach leaves and stock to the pan. Turn up the heat and cook until the dish is piping hot and the stock reduces.

5 Add the rice to the pan. Combine well, season and serve immediately.

CHEFS NOTE
Chicken and paprika make a lovely combination. Prawns also work well with this recipe.

GINGER CHICKEN & ASPARAGUS NOODLES

440 calories per serving

Ingredients

- 200g/7oz asparagus tips
- 200g/7oz cooked chicken breast
- 1 tbsp olive oil
- 1 tsp crushed garlic
- 2 tsp sliced ginger
- 75g/3oz chopped onion
- 2 tbsp soy sauce
- 75g/3oz spinach leaves
- 60ml/¼ cup chicken stock
- 300g/11oz straight-to-wok wholemeal egg noodles
- Salt & pepper to taste

Method

1 Roughly chop the asparagus tips. Cut the cooked chicken breast into strips.

2 Heat the olive oil in a frying pan or wok and gently sauté the garlic, ginger & onions for a few minutes until softened.

3 Add the sliced chicken, soy sauce, spinach, stock & noodles and continue to cook until the dish is piping hot and the stock has reduced.

4 Season & serve.

CHEFS NOTE
Add more garlic & ginger to this dish to suit your own taste.

SESAME OIL STEAK STIR-FRY

480
calories per serving

Ingredients

- 1 red pepper
- 250g/9oz sirloin steak
- 1 tbsp sesame oil
- 125g/4oz trimmed green beans
- 125g/4oz chopped onions
- 1 tsp chopped ginger
- 1 tsp chopped garlic

- 2 tbsp lime juice
- ½ tsp crushed chilli flakes
- 2 tbsp soy sauce
- 250g/9oz ready-to-go microwaveable wholemeal rice
- Salt & pepper to taste

Method

1 De-seed & slice the red pepper. Trim the steak of any fat & slice into strips.

2 Heat the sesame oil in a frying pan or wok and gently sauté the red pepper, green beans, chopped onion, garlic and ginger for a few minutes until softened.

3 Add the lime juice, chilli flakes & soy sauce and continue to cook whilst you microwave the rice.

4 Add the sliced steak to the pan and fry on a high heat for 1-2 minutes or until the steak is cooked to your liking.

5 Add the rice to the pan and combine well. Season and serve.

CHEFS NOTE
Lime wedges to garnish give a sharp twist to this dish.

THAI RED CURRY CHICKEN

460
calories per
serving

Ingredients

- 200g/7oz cooked chicken breast
- 1 tbsp olive oil
- 75g/3oz sliced onion
- 1 tbsp Thai red curry paste
- 1 tbsp lime juice
- 1 tbsp soy sauce
- 75g/3oz watercress
- 300g/11oz straight-to-wok wholemeal egg noodles
- Bunch spring onions/scallions
- Salt & pepper to taste

Method

1 Slice the cooked chicken breast into strips.

2 Heat the olive oil in a frying pan and gently sauté the onion for a few minutes until softened.

3 Add the Thai curry paste, lime juice, soy sauce & chicken and cook for a few minutes.

4 Add noodles and continue to cook until the dish is piping hot.

5 Slice the spring onions and use to garnish your meal.

CHEFS NOTE
You could use also use freshly chopped coriander to garnish this dish.

EGG CURRY

460
calories per
serving

Ingredients

- 4 large free-range eggs
- 1 tsp crushed garlic
- 125g/4oz sliced onions
- 1 tbsp olive oil
- 125g/4oz spinach leaves
- 2 tsp curry powder

- 120ml/½ cup low fat coconut milk
- 1 tbsp tomato puree/paste
- 250g/9oz ready-to-go microwaveable wholemeal rice
- Salt & pepper to taste

Method

1 Hard boil the eggs for 5-7 minutes.

2 Whilst the eggs are boiling, gently sauté the garlic and onions in the olive oil for a few minutes until softened.

3 Roughly chop the spinach and stir through the sautéed onion along with the tomato puree and curry powder. Add the coconut milk and warm though.

4 When the eggs are hardboiled peel and cut in half. Gently place the egg halves, yolk side up, in the coconut milk.

5 Meanwhile microwave the rice and when everything is piping hot, spoon the curry on top of the rice and serve.

CHEFS NOTE

Eggs are widely used in Indian curries. Garnish with chopped parsley or coriander if you wish.

HOMEMADE AVOCADO TOPPED BURGER

440 calories per serving

Ingredients

- 250g/9oz lean beef mince
- 1 tbsp fresh breadcrumbs
- 1 large free-range egg
- 1 tsp crushed garlic
- 1 tsp Dijon mustard
- 1 avocado

- 1 large plum tomato
- 1 handful salad leaves
- 2 wholemeal bread rolls
- Low cal cooking oil spray
- Salt & pepper to taste

Method

1 Preheat the grill.

2 Put the beef mince, breadcrumbs, egg, garlic & mustard in a food processor and pulse for a few seconds to combine.

3 Season well and shape into 2 large burger patties. Spray with a little low cal oil and place under the grill to cook for 5-6 minutes each side or until cooked through.

4 Meanwhile stone & peel the avocado. Slice the avocado flesh and slice the tomato.

5 Split the rolls and when the burgers are cooked through place in a split roll. Lay the sliced tomatoes & avocado on top of the burger along with the salad leaves.

6 Season and serve.

CHEFS NOTE

Its worth buying a plastic burger maker to make perfect burger shapes. They cost very little and really improve the homemade burgers you make.

SPRING GREEN PENNE

440 calories per serving

Ingredients

- 125g/4oz lean, back bacon
- 150g/5oz wholemeal penne
- 1 tbsp olive oil
- 1 tsp crushed garlic
- ½ tsp dried thyme

- 200g/7oz shredded spring greens
- 60ml/¼ cup stock
- 1 tbsp grated Parmesan
- Salt & pepper to taste

Method

1 First trim and finely chop the bacon.

2 Cook the penne in a pan of salted boiling water until tender.

3 Meanwhile heat the olive oil in a high-sided frying pan and gently sauté the bacon pieces & garlic for 3-4 minutes. Add the thyme, spring greens & stock and cook until the greens are tender and the stock has reduced.

4 Drain the cooked penne and add to the frying pan.

5 Toss well and serve with the grated Parmesan sprinkled on top.

CHEFS NOTE
Bags of shredded spring greens are available in most supermarkets. Discard any thick stalks.

FRESH TOMATO & CAPER FUSILLI

390
calories per serving

Ingredients

- 200g/7oz vine ripened tomatoes
- 1 tbsp capers
- 1 tbsp sultanas
- 150g/5oz wholemeal fusilli
- 1 tbsp olive oil

- 2 tsp crushed garlic
- 1 tbsp tomato puree/paste
- 4 tbsp freshly chopped basil
- Salt & pepper to taste

Method

1 Roughly chop the tomatoes, capers & sultanas.

2 Cook the fusilli in a pan of salted boiling water until tender.

3 Meanwhile heat the olive oil in a high-sided frying pan and gently sauté the garlic, chopped tomatoes, capers, sultanas and tomato puree whilst the pasta cooks.

4 Drain the cooked pasta and add to the frying pan.

5 Toss well and serve with the chopped basil on top.

CHEFS NOTE
Reserve a little of the pasta water to stir through & loosen the finished dish.

SERVES 2

GREEK CHICKEN SALAD

400
calories per
serving

Ingredients

- 250g/9oz cooked chicken breast
- 2 large plum tomatoes
- 75g/3oz pitted black olives
- ½ cucumber
- 1 large romaine lettuce
- 100g/3½oz low fat feta cheese

- 1 avocado
- 2 tbsp extra virgin olive oil
- 2 tsp balsamic vinegar
- 1 tsp dried oregano
- Salt & pepper to taste

Method

1 Slice the chicken breast into strips and season.

2 Slice the tomatoes, half the olives and dice the cucumber. Shred the romaine lettuce and cube the feta cheese.

3 De-stone, peel & slice the avocado.

4 Mix together the olive oil, balsamic vinegar and oregano.

5 Toss all the ingredients together in a large bowl.

6 Divide onto plates, check the seasoning and serve.

CHEFS NOTE
You could also add a little lemon juice to the salad if you like.

SWEET MUSTARD CHICKEN PASTA

480
calories per
serving

Ingredients

- 200g/7oz cooked chicken breast
- 150g/5oz wholemeal penne
- 1 tbsp low fat mayonnaise
- 1 tsp runny honey

- 1 tsp Dijon mustard
- 4 tbsp freshly chopped basil
- 1 tbsp Parmesan shavings
- Salt & pepper to taste

Method

1 Cut the chicken breast into slices.

2 Cook the penne in a pan of salted boiling water until tender.

3 Meanwhile mix together the mayonnaise, honey & mustard.

4 Drain the cooked pasta and mix with the honey mayonnaise.

5 Toss well and serve with the sliced, cold chicken on top, sprinkled with Parmesan shavings.

CHEFS NOTE

Using shaved Parmesan gives the dish a different texture but go ahead and use two teaspoons of grated Parmesan if that's all you have to hand.

CREAMY CHICKEN TAGLIATELLE

495 calories per serving

Ingredients

- 200g/7oz cooked chicken breast
- 75g/3oz lean, back bacon
- 150g/5oz wholemeal tagliatelle
- 1 free-range egg
- 1 tbsp olive oil
- 120ml/½ cup low fat crème fraiche
- 1 tbsp grated Parmesan
- Salt & pepper to taste

Method

1 First roughly chop the chicken breast meat. Trim & finely chop the bacon.

2 Cook the tagliatelle in a pan of salted boiling water until tender.

3 Meanwhile gently heat the olive oil in a high-sided frying pan and sauté the pancetta, & chopped chicken whilst the pasta cooks.

4 Lightly beat together the egg and crème fraiche and put to one side.

5 Drain the tagliatelle and add to the frying pan along with the egg & crème fraiche

6 Stir well for 1 minute, remove from the heat and serve.

CHEFS NOTE

The egg and crème fraiche should give a lovely creamy sauce. Single cream is traditionally used for this recipe but will push up the calories count significantly.

SWEET SALMON & ASPARAGUS RICE

420
calories per serving

Ingredients

- 2 boneless, skinless salmon fillets (approx. 125g/4oz each)
- 1 tbsp runny honey
- 1 tbsp soy sauce
- 1 tsp olive oil
- 150g/5oz asparagus tips

- 250g/9oz ready-to-go microwaveable wholemeal rice
- 2 tbsp freshly chopped flat leaf parsley
- Lemon wedges to serve
- Salt & pepper to taste

Method

1 Preheat the grill.

2 Mix together the honey, soy sauce & olive oil. Quickly brush the asparagus tips and salmon fillets in the sticky oil.

3 Place under the grill and cook for 10-13 minutes or until the salmon fillets are cooked through (the asparagus tips should be ready a bit sooner).

4 Whilst the prawns are cooking, microwave the rice. As soon as the asparagus is ready take it out from under the grill roughly chop and toss with the cooked rice.

5 Divide the rice into bowls and serve with the cooked sweet salmon on top.

6 Sprinkle with parsley and serve with lemon wedges.

CHEFS NOTE

You could also try using sweet chilli sauce rather than honey for this recipe.

SIMPLE TUNA SUPPER

490 calories per serving

Ingredients

- 75g/3oz sliced onions
- 1 tbsp sundried tomato puree/paste
- 1 tbsp olive oil
- 150g/5oz fresh peas
- 250g/9oz tinned no drain tuna steak
- 200g/7oz tinned chopped tomatoes
- 1 tsp crushed chilli flakes
- 300g/11oz straight-to-wok wholemeal egg noodles
- 100g/3½oz low fat grated cheddar cheese
- Salt & pepper to taste

Method

1 Preheat the grill

2 Gently sauté the onions and sundried tomato puree in the olive oil for a few minutes until softened.

3 Add the fresh peas, tuna, chopped tomatoes, chilli flakes & noodles. Heat through until piping hot.

4 Tip into an oven-proof bowl. Sprinkle with grated cheese and place under the grill and grill until the cheese bubbles and browns on top.

CHEFS NOTE
Use frozen peas if you like but cook them for a few minutes before adding to the tuna mix.

PRAWN KEBABS & MINTED YOGHURT

415 calories per serving

Ingredients

- 1 red pepper
- 1 yellow pepper
- 2 tsp curry powder
- 1 tsp crushed garlic
- 1 tbsp olive oil
- 1 tbsp lemon juice
- 300g/11oz shelled king prawns

- 250g/9oz ready-to-go microwaveable wholemeal rice
- 3 tbsp fat free Greek yoghurt
- 1 tsp mint sauce
- 4 kebab sticks
- Salt & pepper to taste

Method

1 Preheat the grill.

2 De-seed and cut the peppers into chunks

3 In a large bowl mix together the curry powder, garlic, olive oil & lemon juice.

4 Add the peppers and prawns to the bowl and mix well to coat each piece with the oil mix.

5 Place the pepper pieces and prawns in turn on the skewers. Place the skewers under the grill and cook for 7-10 minutes or until cooked through.

6 Whilst the prawns are cooking, microwave the rice and mix together the yoghurt & mint. Divide the rice into bowls and serve with the cooked skewers on top and the minted yoghurt on the side.

CHEFS NOTE

If you use wooden skewers you will need to pre-soak them in water so that they don't burn.

SPICED CALAMARI

420 calories per serving

Ingredients

- 1 red pepper
- 300g/11oz fresh thin squid rings
- 2 tsp paprika
- 75g/3oz sliced onions
- 2 tsp crushed garlic
- 1 tbsp olive oil
- 2 tbsp soy sauce
- 1 tbsp fish sauce
- 1 tbsp lemon juice
- 250g/9oz straight-to-wok wholemeal egg noodles
- Salt & pepper to taste

Method

1 De-seed and slice the red pepper. Dust the squid with the paprika and season well.

2 Gently sauté the sliced peppers, onions & garlic in the olive oil for a few minutes until softened.

3 Increase the heat and add the squid. Stir-fry for approx. 2 minutes or until the squid is cooked through.

4 Quickly add the soy sauce, fish sauce, lemon juice and noodles. Cook just long enough to heat the noodles through & serve immediately.

CHEFS NOTE
It's really important not to overcook the squid as it can become tough and rubbery.

EXPRESS KEDEGREE

445
calories per
serving

Ingredients

- 2 large free-range eggs
- 1 tbsp olive oil
- 250g/9oz ready-to-go microwaveable wholemeal rice
- 2 tsp curry powder

- 1 tsp crushed garlic
- 2 boneless, skinless smoked haddock fillets (approx. 125g/4oz each)
- 4 tbsp freshly chopped flat leaf parsley
- Salt & pepper to taste

Method

1 Preheat the grill & put the eggs in a saucepan to hard boil (which will take about 4-5 mins after the water starts boiling hard).

2 While the eggs are cooking, season the fish fillets and brush with a little of the oil. Place under the grill and cook for approx. 5 minutes each side or until the fish is cooked through.

3 Meanwhile microwave the rice. When the rice is ready put to one side with the grilled fish.

4 Gently flake the fish. Plunge the eggs in cold water and peel. Cut each egg into quarters. Mix the curry powder and the rest of the olive oil together to make a paste and combine this really well in a bowl with the cooked rice.

5 Gently fold in the flaked haddock and egg quarters.

6 Season and serve.

CHEFS NOTE
You can make this even speedier by having hard-boiled eggs ready in the fridge.

CHORIZO & PEA GNOCCHI

430
calories per
serving

Ingredients

- 125g/5oz chorizo sausage
- 1 tbsp olive oil
- 1 tsp crushed garlic
- 350g/11oz gnocchi

- 250ml/1 cup tomato passata
- 1 tsp each sea salt & brown sugar
- 125g/4oz fresh peas
- Salt & pepper to taste

Method

1 Finely chop the chorizo sausage while you heat the olive oil in a frying pan. Gently sauté the chorizo and garlic in the oil for a few minutes

2 Whilst the onions are softening place the gnocchi in a pan of salted boiling water. Cook for 2-3 minutes or until the gnocchi begins to float to the top.

3 Meanwhile add the passata, sugar, salt & peas to the frying pan.

4 As soon as the gnocchi is cooked, drain and place in the frying pan with everything else. Move the gnocchi around for a few minutes to coat each dumpling in the sauce

5 Check the seasoning and serve.

CHEFS NOTE
If you want the peas to be very soft, add them to the simmering gnocchi for a minute or two before they go into the passata pan.

CHICKEN & MOZZARELLA SALAD

440 calories per serving

Ingredients

- 250g/9oz cooked chicken breast
- 6 large plum tomatoes
- 75g/3oz pitted black olives
- 125g/4oz low fat mozzarella cheese
- 1 ciabatta roll
- ½ tsp crushed garlic

- ½ tsp Dijon mustard
- 1 tbsp balsamic vinegar
- 2 tbsp extra virgin olive oil
- 75g/3oz sliced red onions
- 2 tbsp freshly chopped basil
- Salt & pepper to taste

Method

1 Slice the chicken breast into strips. Slice the tomatoes and half the olives. Drain the mozzarella cheese and cut into 6.

2 Half the ciabatta roll and slice into 2cm wide fingers. Put to one side.

3 In a bowl mix together the garlic, mustard, balsamic vinegar & olive oil along with some salt & pepper. Add the onions to the bowl and combine well.

4 Arrange the chicken, tomatoes, olives and cheese onto the plates.

5 Divide the dressed onions over the top of the salad drizzling any left over juices.

6 Sprinkle with chopped basil and serve with the ciabatta fingers on the side.

CHEFS NOTE

Toast the ciabatta if you want the 'fingers' to have a little crunch to them.

STEAK & FETA SALAD

390 calories per serving

Ingredients

- 250g/9oz sirloin steak
- 2 tbsp olive oil
- 1 red pepper
- 4 large plum tomatoes
- 125g/4oz low fat feta cheese
- ½ tsp crushed chilli flakes
- 1 tsp crushed garlic
- 125g/4oz sliced red onions
- 125g/4oz rocket leaves
- Salt & pepper to taste

Method

1 Trim any fat off the steak. Lightly brush with a little of the olive oil, season and put a frying pan on a high heat.

2 While the pan is heating up de-seed and slice the red pepper. Roughly chop the tomatoes & crumble the feta cheese.

3 Place the steak in the smoking-hot dry pan and cook for 1-2 minutes each side, or to your liking. When the steak is cooked put to one side to rest.

4 Combine together the peppers, tomatoes, crumbled feta cheese, chilli, garlic, onions & remaining olive oil. Arrange on a bed of rocket leaves.

5 Slice the rested steak very thinly and place on top of the feta salad.

6 Season and serve.

CHEFS NOTE
The steak will be medium rare. Cook for a little longer if you prefer.

CONVERSION CHART: DRY INGREDIENTS

Metric	Imperial
7g	¼ oz
15g	½ oz
20g	¾ oz
25g	1 oz
40g	1½oz
50g	2oz
60g	2½oz
75g	3oz
100g	3½oz
125g	4oz
140g	4½oz
150g	5oz
165g	5½oz
175g	6oz
200g	7oz
225g	8oz
250g	9oz
275g	10oz
300g	11oz
350g	12oz
375g	13oz
400g	14oz

Metric	Imperial
425g	15oz
450g	1lb
500g	1lb 2oz
550g	1¼lb
600g	1lb 5oz
650g	1lb 7oz
675g	1½lb
700g	1lb 9oz
750g	1lb 11oz
800g	1¾lb
900g	2lb
1kg	2¼lb
1.1kg	2½lb
1.25kg	2¾lb
1.35kg	3lb
1.5kg	3lb 6oz
1.8kg	4lb
2kg	4½lb
2.25kg	5lb
2.5kg	5½lb
2.75kg	6lb

CONVERSION CHART: LIQUID MEASURES

Metric	Imperial	US
25ml	1fl oz	
60ml	2fl oz	¼ cup
75ml	2½ fl oz	
100ml	3½fl oz	
120ml	4fl oz	½ cup
150ml	5fl oz	
175ml	6fl oz	
200ml	7fl oz	
250ml	8½ fl oz	1 cup
300ml	10½ fl oz	
360ml	12½ fl oz	
400ml	14fl oz	
450ml	15½ fl oz	
600ml	1 pint	
750ml	1¼ pint	3 cups
1 litre	1½ pints	4 cups

Other
TITLES

If you enjoyed **The Healthy Medic Food For Life** recipe book
you may also be interested in other healthy titles
in the series.

LOSE WEIGHT FOR GOOD

THE FAST DIET
FOR BEGINNERS

WEIGHT LOSS WITH INTERMITTENT FASTING

CookNation

NEW
UPCOMING
BESTSELLER

LOSE
WEIGHT
FOR GOOD

BLOOD SUGAR DIET
FOR BEGINNERS

Delicious
Low Calorie
Low Carb
Mediterannean
Style Recipes

CookNation

CookNation

LOSE WEIGHT FOR GOOD

THE KETO DIET

FOR BEGINNERS

COMPLETE KETOGENIC GUIDE TO FAST WEIGHT LOSS WITH LOW CARB, HIGH FAT RECIPES

LOSE WEIGHT FOR GOOD
THE DIET BIBLE

101 Lasting Weight Loss Ideas For Success

CookNation